Writers and Their Work: No. 10

BYRON

by

HERBERT READ

PUBLISHED FOR
THE BRITISH COUNCIL
and the NATIONAL BOOK LEAGUE
by LONGMANS, GREEN & CO.

Revised Price
2s. 6d. net

Sir Herbert Read is one of the most interesting and influential critical writers now living. His reputation is international, and has been built up by twenty-five years of creative writing and of outstanding work in the discussion of both literature and art.

Sir Herbert is a Yorkshireman. He was born in 1893, studied at Leeds University, and fought with distinction as an infantry officer in the First World War, winning the D.S.O. and M.C. After the war he was soon recognized as a poet, and *Mutations of the Phoenix* is probably the best known of his early books. Meanwhile he became associated with T. S. Eliot in the search for more profound and serious values in literary criticism. He was a leading contributor to the *Criterion* during the 1920's, although his views were often distinct from those of T. S. Eliot, the editor.

His *English Prose Style* and his Clark Lectures on Wordsworth consolidated his reputation as a critic; he was pioneer in bringing modern psychological knowledge to bear on literary criticism, though this is only one characteristic in his broad and varied achievement.

In the field of aesthetic criticism Sir Herbert has also become famous. For a generation his name has been known for his exposition of living and contemporary values in art, which he has based on far-ranging historical studies. In recent years his *Education through Art* has established a systematic study of the connexion between the development of personality and its expression in visual art.

In addition to being the author of many books, creative and critical, Sir Herbert was for some time an Assistant Keeper at the Victoria and Albert Museum. He has also been Professor of Fine Art at Edinburgh University and editor of the *Burlington Magazine*. For an appreciation of his work as a writer, the reader is referred to *Herbert Read* by Francis Berry, which is No. 45 in the present series.

Bibliographical Series
of *Supplements to* 'British Book News'

*

GENERAL EDITOR
Bonamy Dobrée

BYRON

From a marble bust of 1822, by BARTOLINI, *in the
National Portrait Gallery*

BYRON

By HERBERT READ

PUBLISHED FOR
THE BRITISH COUNCIL
and the NATIONAL BOOK LEAGUE
BY LONGMANS, GREEN & CO., LONDON, NEW YORK, TORONTO

LONGMANS, GREEN & CO. LTD.
6 & 7 Clifford Street, London W.1
Boston House, Strand Street, Cape Town
531 Little Collins Street, Melbourne

LONGMANS, GREEN & CO. INC.
55 Fifth Avenue, New York 3

LONGMANS, GREEN & CO.
20 Cranfield Road, Toronto 16

ORIENT LONGMANS LTD.
Calcutta Bombay Madras
Delhi Vijayawada Dacca

First published in 1951
Reprinted 1955

Printed in Great Britain at The Curwen Press, Plaistow, E.13

It was evident that he was a prey to some cureless disquiet; but whether it arose from ambition, love, remorse, grief, from one or all of these, or merely from a morbid temperament akin to disease, I could not discover: there were circumstances alleged which might have justified the application to each of these causes; but, as I have before said, these were so contradictory and contradicted, that none could be fixed upon with accuracy. Where there is mystery, it is generally supposed that there must also be evil: I know not how this may be, but in him there certainly was the one, though I could not ascertain the extent of the other—and felt loth, as far as regarded himself, to believe in its existence.

From a Fragment of a Novel by Byron

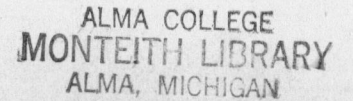

¶ LORD BYRON was born in London on 22 January 1788. He died at Missolonghi on 19 April 1824.

BYRON

THE only hope of treating Byron's life and work with any degree of freshness is to return to the poems, letters, and other personal records. If we then keep our critical attention fixed on the original documents, we may find it possible to ignore most of the commentaries, partial judgements, and subsidiary scandals which for more than a hundred years have obscured the real issues. For these are primarily poetical: Byron intended from his boyhood to be a poet, proceeded to write several substantial volumes of verse, and even during his lifetime was acclaimed a universal genius. At the same time, owing to various incidental features of his life—his social rank, his personal beauty, his numerous love affairs, his private vices and public virtues—the Byronic legend was invented; and ever since Byron the Poet and Byron the Symbolic Figure have existed side by side in the public imagination, the symbol gradually becoming an excuse for neglecting the poetry, and the poetry an excuse for investing the symbol with false sentiment. In Byron's case, even more than in the comparable cases of Goethe and Shelley, it is necessary to guard against the importation of moral judgements into a literary context; or, conversely, against allowing our literary values to influence, one way or the other, our estimate of the moral significance of the poet's actions. Neither the fact that the poet's love affairs were scandalous, nor the fact that he gave his life to the cause of freedom, has any bearing on the position Byron should occupy in the world of letters. If a moral judgement is relevant, the evidence should be detectable in the poetry itself.

The process by which a poet (or a soldier or a politician) becomes a Symbolic Figure is very obscure. It is due to the congruence of certain qualities in the man and to what, for want of a better term, we usually call the Spirit of the Age (*Zeitgeist*). In the case of a poet, it has little to do with the quality of the poetry. In the Elizabethan age, for example, it is Sir Philip Sidney and not Shakespeare who is the Symbolic Figure. An heroic death seems to put the seal on the transaction, but both Sidney and Byron had in some sense been 'elected' before their deaths—Sidney as a 'natural centre'[1] in a free society, Byron as a free spirit in a conventional society. In the course of this essay we must try to define what we mean by freedom of spirit, but whatever its nature, it combined effectively with another quality which Byron possessed, and which was poignantly representative of the period—his *Weltschmerz*.

This peculiar amalgam of naturalistic sentiment, cosmic anxiety, and dispositional spleen had its origin, as its name indicates, in Germany, and Goethe's *Werther* had been its typical embodiment. To what extent *Weltschmerz* was (and still is) an infectious complaint is not in doubt. Though he could not read German (but only swear 'potently' in it), Byron nevertheless held the older poet in great esteem—both *Manfred* and the *Deformed Transformed* are influenced by *Faust*, and *Werner* is dedicated to Goethe.[2] But Byron's own *Weltschmerz* was genuine enough—unless we are to accept the view that his whole life was an affected pose. The clearest expression of the mood is perhaps that given in his Clarens Journal under the date 29 September 1816:

> I am a lover of Nature and an admirer of Beauty. I can bear fatigue and welcome privation, and have seen some of the noblest views in the world. But in all this—the recollections of bitterness, and more especially of recent and more home desolation, which must accompany me through life, have preyed upon me here;

[1] '... he was such a master, with so commending and yet equal ways amongst men, that wheresoever he went, he was beloved and obeyed: yea into what action soever he came last at the first, he became first at the last: the whole managing of the business, not by usurpation or violence, but—as it were—by right and acknowledgment, falling into his hands as into a natural centre.'—Fulke Greville, Lord Brooke.

[2] 'I mean to dedicate Werner to Goethe. I look upon him as the greatest genius that the age has produced. I desired Murray to inscribe his name to a former work; but he pretends my letter containing the order came too late. It would have been more worthy of him than this.' —Thomas Medwin, *Conversations* (1824), p. 329.

and neither the music of the Shepherd, the crashing of the Avalanche, nor the torrent, the mountain, the Glacier, the Forest, nor the Cloud, have for one moment lightened the weight upon my heart, nor enabled me to lose my own wretched identity in the majesty, and the power, and the Glory, around, above, and beneath me.

I am past reproaches; and there is a time for all things. I am past the wish of vengeance, and I know of none like for what I have suffered; but the hour will come, when what I feel must be felt, and the —— but enough.

Letters and Journals, III, 364-5

This particular Journal was written for Augusta, 'my own dearest Sis', with whom he was always as unaffected as it was in his nature to be, and we may assume that Byron really did feel and suffer in this way. Our first task should be an attempt at a diagnosis of his state of mind, for out of it proceeded not only the almost daemonic energy with which he lived and wrote, but also the substance and, in some sense to be determined, the quality of what he wrote.

We have been taught to look in two places for a clue to a person's temperament—in heredity and in early environment. In both Byron was exceptional. His ancestors on both sides were for the most part bold, lawless, and dissolute, and to call them aristocratic is to dignify a clan that was only exclusive in its barbarism. Their violence of temper was obviously neurotic and was expressed, not only in various types of manslaughter, legal or illegal, but occasionally also in suicide—it has been suggested that even his father, 'mad Jack Byron', committed suicide.[1] The eccentricities and extravagances of these gentry are fully recorded in various biographical works, but here we need only consider Byron's own attitude to his heritage. It is clearly expressed in a letter he wrote to a Monsieur J. J. Coulmann who published an account of a visit he paid to Byron in Genoa in 1823:

[1] The suggestion, said to come from Byron himself, may be traced back to the Rev. William Harness, who as a boy was befriended by Byron at Harrow. It is repeated by Jeaffreson (vol. 1, p. 45) and Maurois (Eng. trans., p. 33) but has no documentary basis.

Byron is writing to correct certain statements published by a Monsieur Pichot in an essay attached to the fourth edition of a translation of his *Oeuvres complètes* which Coulmann had sent to him:

> ... the same author has cruelly calumniated my father and my grand-uncle, but more especially the former. So far from being 'brutal', he was, according to the testimony of all those who knew him, of an extremely amiable and (*enjoué*) joyous character, but careless (*insouciant*) and dissipated. He had, consequently, the reputation of a good officer, and showed himself such in the Guards, in America. The facts themselves refute the assertion. It is not by 'brutality' that a young Officer in the Guards seduces and carries off a Marchioness, and marries two heiresses. It is true that he was a very handsome man, which goes a great way. . . . His second wife, my respected mother, had, I assure you, too proud a spirit to bear the ill-usage of any man, no matter who he might be; and this she would have soon proved. I should add, that he lived a long time in Paris, and was in habits of intimacy with the old Marshal Biron, Commandant of the French Guards; who, from the similitude of names, and Norman origin of our family, supposed that there was some distant relationship between us. He died some years before the age of forty, and whatever may have been his faults, they were certainly not those of harshness and grossness (*dureté et grossierté*) . . . Augusta and I have always loved the memory of our father as much as we loved each other, and this at least forms a presumption that the stain of harshness was not applicable to it.[1]

Byron was only three years old when in the summer of 1791 his father died at Valenciennes, whither he had fled some months earlier. Even allowing for the child's precocity, his knowledge of his father's character could not have been very direct. But there is no doubt that in his fatherless state, and in reaction to his mother, Byron developed a mental 'complex' of a specific kind. Of his mother he wrote, at the age of sixteen, the following account:

[1] *Letters and Journals*, VI, 231–2. The letter, though probably written in English by Byron, was published in French and subsequently re-translated to English by another hand.

MY DEAREST AUGUSTA,—I seize this interval of my *amiable* mother's absence this afternoon, again to inform you, or rather to be informed by you, of what is going on. For my own part I can send nothing to amuse you, excepting a repetition of my complaints against my tormentor, whose *diabolical* disposition (pardon me for staining my paper with so harsh a word) seems to increase with age, and to acquire new force with Time. The more I see of her the more my dislike augments; nor can I so entirely conquer the appearance of it, as to prevent her from perceiving my opinion; this, so far from calming the Gale, blows it into a *hurricane*, which threatens to destroy everything, till exhausted by its own violence, it is lulled into a sullen torpor, which, after a short period, is again roused into fresh and revived frenzy, to me most terrible, and to every other Spectator astonishing. She then declares that she plainly sees I hate her, that I am leagued with her bitter enemies, viz. Yourself, Ld C[arlisle] and Mr. H[anson], and, as I never Dissemble or contradict her, we are all *honoured* with a multiplicity of epithets, too *numerous*, and some of them too *gross*, to be repeated. . . . Such Augusta is the happy life I now lead, such my *amusements*. I wander about hating everything I behold, and if I remained here a few months longer, I should become, what with *envy, spleen and all uncharitableness*, a complete *misanthrope*. . . .

Letters and Journals, I, 30–1

There are several other passages to the same effect in Byron's letters, and from them we gather a significant detail —Mrs. Byron was in the habit of 'raking up the ashes of my *father*'. 'Within one little hour, I have not only heard myself, but have heard my *whole family*, by the father's side, *stigmatized* in terms that the *blackest malevolence* would perhaps shrink from, and that too in words that you would be shocked to hear. Such, Augusta, such is my mother; *my mother!*' It needs no elaborate psychological reasoning to see that such a situation was bound to give rise to an idealization of the lost parent—even, in the technical Freudian sense, to an identification, and therefore to a powerful element in the formation of Byron's character. 'Mad Jack', with all his amiable and joyous habits, became the beau idéal (we now call it the ego-ideal) of the young Byron.

Among other possible influences of a decisive character in Byron's formative years, one must pause a little curiously over the name of May Gray, his Scottish 'nannie'. She was with him from earliest infancy until the end of 1799—that is to say, for the first twelve years of his life. Considering the character of his mother, it is likely that this unknown woman obtained a considerable hold upon the imagination of her charge. She seems to have combined a superstitious Calvinism with a more natural profligacy, and when John Hanson, the Byrons' solicitor, visited Nottingham in 1799, during the absence of Mrs. Byron, he was so appalled by the relationship that then existed between the servant and her charge that he wrote to Mrs. Byron to suggest instant dismissal. Here is the picture he drew:

> My honourable little companion, tho' disposed to retain his feelings, could not refrain, from the harsh usage he had received at her hands, from complaining to me, and such is his dread of the Woman that I really believe he would forego the satisfaction of seeing you if he thought he was not to meet her again. He told me that she was perpetually beating him, and that his bones sometimes ached from it; that she brought all sorts of Company of the very lowest Description into his apartments; that she was out late at nights, and he was frequently left to put himself to bed; that she would take the Chaise-boys into the Chaise with her, and stopped at every little Ale-house to drink with them. But, Madam, this is not all; she has even—traduced yourself.
>
> *Letters and Journals*, I, 10 n.

Byron was then eleven years old, and all of them had been spent in close association with this woman. It is a speculation, of course, but it would seem likely that she had some connexion with those early and fatal experiences to which Byron made frequent and mysterious reference. 'My passions were developed very early,' he wrote in the journal of 1821 which he called 'Detached Thoughts'—'so early, that few would believe me, if I were to state the period, and the facts which accompanied it. Perhaps this was one of the reasons which caused the anticipated melancholy of my thoughts—having anticipated life.' And again, in the same journal: 'If I could explain at length the *real* causes which have contributed to increase this perhaps *natural* temperament of mine, this Melancholy which hath made me a bye-word, nobody would wonder; but this is impossible without doing much mischief. I do not know what other men's lives have been, but I cannot conceive anything more strange than some of the earlier parts of mine. I have written my memoirs, but omitted *all* the really *consequential* and *important* parts, from deference to the dead, to the living, and to those who must be both.' It is sometimes suggested that these are exaggerated references to his early passion for Mary Duff (the little girl with whom he fell in love at the age of nine), but that experience must have been innocent enough, and we have Hobhouse's witness to the fact. In a marginal note to Moore's *Life* (first published by Maurois, *Byron*, p. 442) he remarked: 'With respect to the early development of these propensities in Byron, I am acquainted with a regular fact scarcely fit for narration, but much less romantic and more satisfactory than the amour with Mary Duff.' In a letter to Lady Melbourne of 1 May 1814, referring evidently to Augusta, Byron wrote: 'It, indeed, puzzles me to account for ——: it is true she married a fool, but she *would* have him; they agreed, and agree very well, and I have never heard a complaint, but many vindications, of him. As for me, brought up as I was, and sent into the world as I was, both physically and morally, nothing better could be expected, and it is odd that I always had a foreboding and I remember when a child reading the Roman history about a *marriage* I will tell you of when we meet, asking my mère why I should not marry X.' The reference is to his half-sister, Augusta Leigh, and the letter indicates clearly that his early experiences were of a nature demoralizing enough to extenuate, in his own view, his later guilt; and to the same early experiences he always attributed those feelings of melancholy and disgust which drove him to a heartless libertinism. The following description of his life at Cambridge (from 'Detached Thoughts') gives an impression of unaffected self-analysis:

> My companions were not unsocial, but the contrary—lively, hospitable, of rank, and fortune, and gay far beyond my gaiety. I mingled with, and dined and supped, etc., with them; but I know not how, it was one of the deadliest and heaviest feelings of my life to feel that I was no longer a boy. From that moment I began to grow old in my own esteem; and in my esteem age is not estimable. I took my gradations in the vices with great promptitude, but they were not to my taste; for my early passions, though violent in the extreme, were concentrated, and hated division or spreading abroad. I could have left or lost the world with or for that which I loved; but, though my temperament was naturally burning, I could not share in the common place libertinism of the place and time without disgust. And yet this very disgust, and my heart thrown back upon itself, threw me into excesses perhaps more fatal than those from which I shrunk, as fixing upon one (at a time) the passions, which, spread amongst many, would have hurt only myself.
>
> *Letters and Journals*, V, 445-6

'I must not go on with these reflections', wrote Byron in this same journal of 1821, 'or I shall be letting out some secret or other to paralyse posterity.' He never did let out that secret, and though Hobhouse and one or two other intimate friends may have known it, they too kept silent. Byron in general was not at all squeamish in his conversation, letters, and journals, and it is difficult to imagine the nature of the experience that produced such a permanent psychological trauma. But there is no doubt of its reality—it was no pretence on Byron's part, and its effect was not merely a disgust of life and a heart 'thrown back upon itself', but also an effort to escape from himself which took the form of poetic activity. 'To withdraw *myself* from *myself* (oh that cursed selfishness!) has ever been my sole, my entire, my sincere motive in scribbling at all; and publishing is also the continuance of the same object, by the action it affords to the mind, which else recoils upon itself.'

(*Journal* of 1813.) It is true that about three months earlier (6 September) in sending Miss Milbanke a somewhat artificial portrait of himself he had expressed a somewhat different philosophy of life. 'The great object of life is sensation—to feel that we exist, even though in pain. It is this "craving void" which drives us to gaming—to battle—to travel—to intemperate, but keenly felt pursuits of any description, whose principal attraction is the agitation inseparable from their accomplishment.' But he would hardly venture to exhibit the blackness of his humours to his prospective bride—a 'craving void' she would understand and appreciate: it was the fashionable *Angst* of the period.

Whilst we must admit that Byron's despair was a very real thing, and in some sense the basis of his feverish activity, nevertheless he was inspired by a more naïve sense of glory. Byron at sixteen was not too young to be taken seriously, and at that age he had written to his mother: ' . . . the way *to riches, to greatness* lies before me. I can, I will cut myself a path through the world or perish in the attempt. Others have begun life with nothing and ended greatly. And shall I, who have a competent if not a large fortune, remain idle? No, I will carve myself the passage to Grandeur, but never with Dishonour. These, Madam, are my intentions."[1] And at the other end of his life there is no doubt that he was stirred by the same sense of glory:

> The dead have been awakened—shall I sleep?
> The World's at war with tyrants—shall I crouch?
> The harvest's ripe—and shall I pause to reap?
> I slumber not; the thorn is in my Couch;
> Each day a trumpet soundeth in mine ear,
> Its echo in my heart—[2]

It was a call he responded to—two months later he was in Cephalonia and ten months later he was dead. The wavering ambivalence of his will is expressed in that last poem which

[1] *Byron: a Self-Portrait.* Edited by Peter Quennell. London, 1950, I, 10.
[2] *Letters*, 1901, vi, 238.

has some claim to be considered his best, written on his thirty-sixth birthday:

'T is time this heart should be unmoved,
  Since others it hath ceased to move:
Yet, though I cannot be beloved,
  Still let me love!

My days are in the yellow leaf;
  The flowers and fruits of Love are gone;
The worm, the canker, and the grief
  Are mine alone!

The fire that on my bosom preys
  Is lone as some Volcanic isle;
No torch is kindled at its blaze—
  A funeral pile.

The hope, the fear, the jealous care,
  The exalted portion of the pain
And power of love, I cannot share,
  But wear the chain.

But 't is not *thus*—and 't is not *here*—
  Such thoughts should shake my soul, not *now*
Where Glory decks the hero's bier,
  Or binds his brow.

The Sword, the Banner, and the Field,
  Glory and Greece, around me see!
The Spartan, borne upon his shield,
  Was not more free.

Awake! (not Greece—she *is* awake!)
  Awake, my spirit! Think through *whom*
Thy life-blood tracks its parent lake,
  And then strike home!

Tread those reviving passions down,
  Unworthy manhood!—unto thee
Indifferent should the smile or frown
  Of Beauty be.

> If thou regret'st thy youth, *why live?*
> The land of honourable death
> Is here:—up to the Field, and give
> Away thy breath!
>
> Seek out—less often sought than found—
> A soldier's grave, for thee the best;
> Then look around, and choose thy ground,
> And take thy Rest.

It is almost too good to be true—true in the sense of being authentic, true in the sense of being sincere. But it is both, and it illustrates the contradiction within Byron's personality. In such a case one must recall Lord Acton's profound observation: 'Good and evil lie close together. Seek no artistic unity in character.' If we must accept the word evil to describe one aspect of Byron's character (and certainly we must if we share Acton's morality) then we must also accept the word good to describe this other equally significant aspect. My own view is that Byron was in some sense beyond good and evil, one of Nietzsche's 'free spirits'. But as Nietzsche was careful to point out, that is a privilege given to the very few, and does not arise from a sense of obligation, from vulgar ambition. The kind of aristocracy from which Byron sprang may be eugenically questionable, but at least he had the aristocratic sense of detachment. Complaining to Murray about the books he had sent out to him to read in Ravenna ('Campbell is lecturing, Moore idling, Southey twaddling, Wordsworth driveling, Coleridge muddling, Joanna Baillie piddling, Bowles quibbling, squabbling and sniveling...') he observed: 'The pity of these men is, that they never lived either in *high life*, nor in *solitude*: there is no medium for the knowledge of the *busy* or the *still* world. If admitted into high life for a season, it is merely as *spectators*—they form no part of the Mechanism thereof. Now Moore and I, the one by circumstances, and the other by birth, happened to be free of the corporation, and to have entered into its pulses and passions, *quarum partes fuimus*. Both of us have learnt by this much which nothing else could have taught us.' (*Letters and Journals*, V, 362-3.) That he could admit Moore, the son of an Irish grocer, into the same class proves that his conception of aristocracy was not altogether snobbish. The further notion that it belongs to the still world no less than to the busy world shows that the conception was not merely social and superficial. Byron was always conscious of his obligations and responsibilities—personal obligations to his friends and dependants, public responsibilities towards the poor and oppressed. These feelings were not sympathetic: they were based on his concept of justice and his confident knowledge that he had 'a part to play' in the world.

There are perhaps only two other aspects of his personality that need be mentioned—the quality of his affections, and the quality of his intelligence. His attitude to women is too notorious to need much discussion. There is no doubt that he had a strong and perhaps unconscious need for the maternal affection that had been denied to him in childhood, and this was supplied by a friend like Lady Melbourne and also, in some more obscure sense, by Augusta Leigh. 'There is something to me,' he once confessed, 'very softening in the presence of a woman,—some strange influence, even if one is not in love with them—which I cannot at all account for, having no very high opinion of the sex. But yet,—I always feel in better humour with myself and every thing else, if there is a woman within ken. Even Mrs. Mule, my firelighter,—the most ancient and withered of her kind, —and (except to myself) not the best-tempered—always makes me laugh,—no difficult task when I am "i' the vein".' (*Journal*, 27 February 1814.) But the feelings aroused by a Caroline Lamb or a Frances Webster cannot be described as 'very softening'. It is a chase, with the possibility of a kill at the end; and the kill (which may be sadistically prolonged) is the end of the matter so far as Byron himself is concerned. Only towards the end of his life does he begin to tire of the chase and to submit (with Teresa Guiccioli) to something like constant devotion. Even so—'It is awful work, this love, and prevents all a man's projects of good and glory'.

One might pursue the analysis of Byron's amorous propensities into more detail, but it would not add much to our general understanding of the man. He loved as he wrote—to escape from himself. But he loved with discrimination. 'What an antithetical mind!' he cried on reading some 'unpublished and never-to-be-published' letters of Burns's '—tenderness, roughness—delicacy, coarseness—sentiment, sensuality—soaring and grovelling, dirt and deity—all mixed up in that one compound of inspired clay!' That was not his way of life, or of love. 'A true voluptuary', he wrote in his *Journal* (13 December 1813), 'will never abandon his mind to the grossness of reality. It is by exalting the earthly, the material, the *physique* of our pleasures, by veiling these ideas, by forgetting them altogether, or, at least, never naming them hardly to one's self, that we alone can prevent them from disgusting.' It is not on record that any of the women he loved ever regretted the experience.

Byron's intelligence, by which I mean his natural sagacity rather than his intellectual powers, has perhaps never been sufficiently appreciated. His handling of his agents and his publisher was always admirably clear and concise (though not necessarily tactful). Considering the kind of life he wished to lead, he dealt with his estates and debts in a practical and decisive fashion. In Greece he showed a genuine capacity for administration and the logistics of a military campaign. But it is in his daily life—his relationships with his friends and his comments of the events of the day—that we find, not common sense, but sensitive moral perceptions. One has only to follow, in the sequence of letters he wrote to Lady Melbourne, the course of his abortive wooing of Lady Frances Webster, to see in full operation a social strategy, part instinct and part design, which belongs to the highest, if least profitable, of human capacities.

Of Byron's intellectual powers one must speak with less

respect. He was superstitious, but not religious; an atheist, and yet a fatalist. From various sources, as I have already said, he had contracted the current *Weltschmerz*, and in this mood he would sometimes attempt to philosophize—in poetry and in prose. The following sample, from the *Diary* of 1821, gives the substance of it all:

> Why, at the very height of desire and human pleasure,—worldly, social, amorous, ambitious, or even avaricious,—does there mingle a certain sense of doubt and sorrow—a fear of what is to come—a doubt of what *is*—a retrospect to the past, leading to a prognostication of the future? ... I know not, except that on a pinnacle we are most susceptible of giddiness, and that we never fear falling except from a precipice—the higher, the more awful, and the more sublime; and, therefore, I am not sure that Fear is not a pleasurable sensation; at least, *Hope* is; and *what Hope* is there without a deep leaven of Fear? and what sensation is so delightful as Hope? and, if it were not for Hope, where would the Future be?—in hell. It is useless to say *where* the Present is, for most of us know; and as for the Past, *what* predominates in memory?—*Hope baffled*. Ergo, in all human affairs, it is Hope—Hope—Hope. I allow sixteen minutes, though I never counted them, to any given or supposed possession. From whatever place we commence, we know where it all must end. And yet, what good is there in knowing it? It does not make men better or wiser. During the greatest horrors of the greatest plagues (Athens and Florence, for example—see Thucydides and Machiavelli), men were more cruel and profligate than ever. It is all a mystery. I feel most things, but I know nothing, except
>
> — — — — — — — —
> — — — — — — — —
> — — — — — — — —
> — — — — — — — —

Admittedly this becomes more impressive when it is rhymed:

> Between two worlds Life hovers like a star,
>   'Twixt Night and Morn, upon the horizon's verge.
> How little do we know that which we are!
>   How less what we may be! The eternal surge
> Of Time and Tide rolls on and bears afar

> Our bubbles; as the old burst, new emerge,
> Lashed from the foam of ages; while the graves
> Of Empires heave but like some passing waves.[1]

But nothing can disguise the essential emptiness of such a philosophy, and it is merely to dignify emptiness that we call it Nihilism. The philosophical reaction to Nihilism at the beginning of the nineteenth century was to be various forms of Existentialism, but though we can make out a case for regarding Coleridge and Wordsworth as existentialists of this kind, Byron remains obstinately cynical, gaily—but not confidently—superficial.

At this point a Marxist critic would no doubt attempt to relate Byron's state of mind to the profound social changes that were taking place in his time. There he was, representative of an old order (positively feudal!); around him, a new order with which he had no sympathy was coming into being; his very estates were to be sold to make way for the industrial revolution. Vulgarity was everywhere triumphant, and politics authoritarian. All this, to the full extent of a sociological thesis, we can admit; but in the end we have not explained why Byron became a nihilist and Shelley, in the same circumstances, a utopian socialist. In social status, in material environment, in historical destiny, nothing separated these two men; yet the quality of their poetry is totally distinct and their philosophy of life antithetical. They agree only in their revolt from the society into which they were born.

Nevertheless, Shelley was one of the few of his contemporaries whom Byron could admire. In no other direction is the limitation of Byron's intelligence so evident as in his literary judgements. One must admit that they were not consistently wrong, and they were never conventional. He had a real appreciation of Goethe's greatness, and on the basis of an Italian translation one finds him ready to acclaim —surely in advance of any other English critic—the genius

---

[1] *Don Juan*, XV, xcix. 'End of Canto 15th Mch. 25, 1823, B.'

of Grillparzer ('... the tragedy of *Sappho* is superb and sublime! There is no denying it. The man has done a great thing in writing that play. And *who is he*? I know him not; but *ages will*. 'Tis a high intellect... Grillparzer is grand—antique—*not so simple* as the ancients, but very simple for a modern—too Madame de Stael*ish*, now and then—but altogether a great and goodly writer.') (*Diary*, 12 January 1821.) His opinions of past authors have consistency, too, and illustrate his prejudices. 'I look upon a proper appreciation of Pope as a touchstone of taste, and the present question as not only whether Pope is or is not in the first rank of our literature, but whether *that* literature shall or shall not relapse into the Barbarism from which it has scarcely emerged for above a century and a half.' 'It is also a great error', he added, 'to suppose the *present* a *high* age of English poetry. ... Those poor idiots of the Lakes... are diluting out literature as much as they can.' (Letter to Octavius Gilchrist, 5 September 1821. (Quennell: *Byron, a Self-Portrait*, II, 664.)) Those poor idiots included, besides Southey, whom he despised on other than literary grounds, Wordsworth and Coleridge. The early Wordsworth he had admired. Writing to Leigh Hunt (30 October 1815) he said: 'I take leave to differ with you on Wordsworth, as freely as I once agreed with you; at that time I gave him credit for a promise, which is unfulfilled. I still think his capacity warrants all you say of *it* only, but that his performances since *Lyrical Ballads* are miserably inadequate to the ability which lurks within him: there is undoubtedly much natural talent spilt over the *Excursion*; but it is rain upon rocks—where it stands and stagnates, or rain upon sands—where it falls without fertilizing. Who can understand him? Let those who do, make him intelligible. Jacob Behmen, Swedenborg, and Joanna Southcote, are mere types of this arch-apostle of mystery and mysticism.' This makes clear (as his earlier review of the *Poems* of 1807 had done[1]) that Byron's objection to Wordsworth was genuinely critical—he appreciated his 'native

[1] *Letters and Journals*, I, 341-3.

elegance, natural and unaffected', except where it became 'namby-pamby', but he had no sympathy for Wordsworth's philosophic faith, and perhaps no patience with it. But when it came to Keats there was what one can only describe as an organic lack of poetic sensibility in Byron. 'Mr. Keats... appears to me what I have already said: such writing is a sort of mental masturbation—★ ★ ★ ★ ★ ★ ★ ★ his *Imagination*. I don't mean he is *indecent*, but viciously soliciting his own ideas into a state, which is neither poetry nor any thing else but a Bedlam vision produced by raw pork and opium.' (Letter to John Murray, 18 November 1820—best consulted in Quennell, *op. cit.*, p. 536.) Elsewhere he refers to 'the *outstretched* poesy of this miserable Self-polluter of the human mind', and the only clue to an explanation of such violence (for the two men had no personal contacts) is a reference in another letter to Keats's 'abuse of Pope'. To abuse Pope was as good as abusing Byron himself.

In his *Journal* of 1813 Byron drew 'a triangular *Gradus ad Parnassum*'. At the summit, 'undoubtedly the Monarch of Parnassus, and the most *English* of bards', he placed Walter Scott. Next, as 'the last of the *best* school', Rogers; Moore and Campbell both third, followed, a grade lower, by Southey, Wordsworth, and Coleridge; and, below them, 'the Many'. It is true that he adds, as an afterthought: 'I have ranked the names upon my triangle more upon what I believe popular opinion, than any decided opinion of my own', but his own gloss does not make any substantial difference to what we should now regard as a strange lack of discernment—'For, to me, some of Moore's last *Erin* sparks —"As a beam o'er the face of the waters"—"When he who adores thee"—"Oh blame not"—and "Oh breathe not his name"—are worth all the Epics that ever were composed.' All contemporary judgement is liable to aberration, and a critic of today has no grounds for feeling superior to Byron; but we have only to contrast his opinions with those of Shelley or Keats to see how much more sensitive they were to the enduring values in poetry.

This is perhaps to adopt a theory of poetry that Byron himself would not have admitted, and it is the theory upon which we must find Byron's own poetry lacking in certain essential qualities. These qualities may be specifically 'romantic', and my criticism of Byron's poetry must be expressed from within the romantic tradition. This tradition requires, in the highest type of poetry, two qualities which Byron despised—*curiosa felicitas* and ideal beauty. By the former phrase we mean, not merely apt words to express a thought (Byron had them in plenty) but words which by the originality of their application, or the originality of their collocation, produce an essentially somatic thrill of appreciation. The difference is easier to illustrate than to describe. Byron's felicity is at its best in lines such as:

> She walks in beauty like the night
> Of cloudless climes and starry skies.

It is an explicit felicity; no image, no word, is far-fetched; that climes should be cloudless and skies starry is in each case the obvious cliché. But take two comparable lines from Donne:

> No Spring, nor Summer Beauty hath such grace,
> As I have seen in one Autumnal face.

Byron was utterly incapable of using an epithet with such a wealth of implied imagery as 'Autumnal' has in this context. One might say that his mind did not work in that way, and then one has said that his mind was not in the most fundamental sense poetic. He had other qualities, as I shall presently readily admit; but it is useless to pretend that he possessed that absolute grace which we find, not only in major poets like Chaucer, Spenser, Shakespeare, Milton, and Wordsworth; but also in a Wyatt, a Herrick, a Burns, a Hopkins.

As for ideal beauty, by this we mean, in Landor's words, 'the sublimer emanation, I will not say of the real, for this is the more real of the two, but of that which is ordinarily subject to the senses'. Great poets have believed that they were in some way giving expression to something greater than themselves. Wordsworth, for example, believed

> That Poets, even as Prophets, each with each
> Connected in a mighty scheme of truth,
> Have each for his peculiar dower, a sense
> By which he is enabled to perceive
> Something unseen before

and on the basis of this belief, he hoped that a work of his

> Proceeding from the depth of untaught things,
> Enduring and creative, might become
> A power like one of Nature's.

To such a claim Byron would have answered with a hoot of derision. Reality, and any thought about reality, was precisely what he wished to avoid. 'I began a comedy, and burnt it because the scene ran into *reality*—a novel, for the same reason. In rhyme, I can keep more away from the facts; but the thought always runs through, through ... yes, yes, through.' And, from the same 'log-book' (1813): 'I envy no one the certainty of his self-approved wisdom.' It was not merely that Byron had no ambition to give expression to a philosophical faith in his verse—as we have seen, he had none that was worth the trouble; rather, he regarded the practice of verse-writing as a means of 'getting rid of thinking'. This attitude is not to be confused with superficiality, or shallowness of thought. It is a consciously adopted sophistication; a positive belief in making life an amusement and verse-writing a playful artifice. In self-criticism he found himself failing to live up to this ideal:

> With regard to poetry in general, I am convinced, the more I think of it, that he (Moore) and *all* of us—Scott, Southey, Wordsworth, Moore, Campbell, I,—are all in the wrong, one as much as another; that we are upon a wrong revolutionary poetical system, or systems, not worth a damn in itself, and from which none but

Rogers and Crabbe are free; and that the present and next generations will finally be of this opinion. I am the more confirmed in this by having lately gone over some of our classics, particularly *Pope*, whom I tried in this way—I took Moore's poems and my own and some others, and went over them side by side with Pope's, and I was really astonished (I ought not to have been so) and mortified at the ineffable distance in point of sense, harmony, effect, and even *Imagination*, passion, and *Invention*, between the little Queen Anne's man, and us of the Lower Empire.

(To John Murray, 17 September 1817),
Letters and Journals, IV, 169

It is the classical point of view, but Byron himself did not possess a classical mind, a disciplined nature. Only a fortnight before he wrote this letter, Byron had finished copying out the final draft of the fourth canto of *Childe Harold's Pilgrimage*, his most romantic poem.

> Oh! that the Desert were my dwelling-place,
>   With one fair Spirit for my minister,
>   That I might all forget the human race,
>   And, hating no one, love but only her!
> Ye elements!—in whose ennobling stir
>   I feel myself exalted—Can ye not
>   Accord me such a Being? Do I err
>   In deeming such inhabit many a spot?
> Though with them to converse can rarely be our lot.
>
> There is a pleasure in the pathless woods,
>   There is a rapture on the lonely shore,
>   There is society, where none intrudes,
>   By the deep Sea, and Music in its roar:
>   I love not Man the less, but Nature more,
>   From these our interviews, in which I steal
>   From all I may be, or have been before,
>   To mingle with the Universe, and feel
> What I can ne'er express—yet can not all conceal.

Romantic and classic—we exchange these counters with bewildering effect. If to steal away and mingle with the Universe is a romantic proceeding, then Byron is the romantic, and Wordsworth and Coleridge, who were always careful to keep logical distinctions between man and nature, were classical. But if to write verse of this ease and suavity is to be classical, then Byron was classical, and the poets of *Kubla Khan* and *Michael* were romantic experimentalists, obsessed with some notion of a correspondency between form and feeling. There is more essential discipline in one of Wordsworth's sonnets ('They are the most puling, petrifying, stupidly platonic compositions', said Byron of sonnets in general) than in the whole of Byron's work. We must deny Byron that classical virtue. On the other hand, we must grant him the true romantic afflatus, the wildest poetic energy in the whole range of post-Shakespearian poetry. And yet writing was for him 'a task, and a painful one'. 'I feel exactly as you do about our "art",' he wrote to Moore, 'but it comes over me in a kind of rage every now and then, like ★ ★ ★ ★, and then, if I don't write to empty my mind, I go mad. As to that regular, uninterrupted love of writing, which you describe in your friend, I do not understand it. I feel it as a torture, which I must get rid of, but never as a pleasure. On the contrary, I think composition a great pain.' He hated revising texts and correcting proofs, and at a pinch was willing that his friends should do the job for him. There are a few faultless lyrics, and there are many stanzas that conform to a pattern; but in general Byron's verse reveals a virtuoso's supreme contempt for the rules of the game, and he is never happier than when he gets by with some outrageous simile or far-fetched rhyme.

> Scherematoff and Chrematoff, Koklophti,
>   Koclobski, Kourakin, and Mouskin Pouskin,
> All proper men of weapons, as e'er scoffed high
>   Against a foe, or ran a sabre through skin:
> Little cared they for Mahomet or Mufti,
>   Unless to make their kettle-drums a new skin. . . .

One of his most famous lyrics ('The Isles of Greece') is introduced with the following couplet:

In Italy he'd ape the 'Trecentisti';
In Greece, he'd sing some sort of hymn like this t'ye:

But these are not faults: they are the deliberate scrabblings of an impressionistic style.[1]

In this style the works of Byron that we still read were written—*Don Juan, Childe Harold, The Vision of Judgment, Beppo*. All these works are satires—'*Don Juan* will be known by and bye, for what it is intended,—a *Satire* on *abuses* of the present states of Society, and not an eulogy of vice: it may be now and then voluptuous: I can't help that'. (Letter to Murray, 25 December 1822.) As such, this poem needs no further praise than that bestowed on it by its author:

> As to *Don Juan*, confess, confess—you dog and be candid—that it is the sublime of *that there* sort of writing—it may be bawdy but is it not good English? It may be profligate but is it not *life*, is it not *the thing*? Could any man have written it who has not lived in the world?—and fooled in a post-chaise?—in a hackney coach?—in a gondola?—against a wall?—in a court carriage?—in a vis-à-vis?—on a table?—and under it?
>
> (Letter to the Hon. Douglas Kinnaird, 26 October 1819.
> Quennell, *op. cit.*, 491)

Yes: the sublime of 'that there sort of writing'—in its class it remains, if not sublime, supreme—more vital, more amusing, more pertinent than anything of colder perfection that his most admired master ever wrote.

When this has been said, there remains the stricture that it is all a heartless and, if not immoral, then amoral exercise of wit, of little use to man or God.[2] Byron himself was well

---

[1] The painterly term is not altogether inappropriate. Reading Byron (in 1824) Eugène Delacroix felt again 'that insatiable desire to create'. It was the beginning of the Impressionist movement in painting.

[2] Cf. Sir Herbert Grierson: 'All that Byron's poem wants is what no writer content to be a satirist and jester only could give it, a deeper pity for the human heart that suffers and is defeated in this strange, meaningless pageant.' Preface to *Poems of Lord Byron*, London (Florence Press), 1923, p. xv.

aware of this criticism and meets it at the beginning of Canto XIII of *Don Juan*. After warning the reader that

> I now mean to be serious;—it is time,
>   Since Laughter now-a-days is deemed too serious;
> A jest at Vice by Virtue's called a crime,
>   And critically held as deleterious . . .

he proceeds to defend himself as the *spectator ab extra*:

> Rough Johnson, the great moralist, professed,
>   Right honestly, 'he liked an honest hater!'—
> The only truth that yet has been confessed
>   Within these latest thousand years or later.
> Perhaps the fine old fellow spoke in jest:—
>   For my own part, I am but a mere spectator,
> And gaze where'er the palace or the hovel is,
> Much in the mode of Goethe's Mephistopheles;
>
> But neither love nor hate in much excess;
>   Though 't was not once so. If I sneer sometimes,
> It is because I cannot well do less,
>   And now and then it also suits my rhymes.
> I should be very willing to redress
>   Men's wrongs, and rather check than punish crimes,
> Had not Cervantes, in that too true tale
> Of Quixote, shown how all such efforts fail.

And after describing Cervantes's tale, he turns to 'the great moral taught by that real Epic unto all who have thought':

> Cervantes smiled Spain's chivalry away;
>   A single laugh demolished the right arm
> Of his own country;—seldom since that day
>   Has Spain had heroes. While Romance could charm,
> The World gave ground before her bright array;
>   And therefore have his volumes done much harm,
> That all their glory, as a composition,
> Was dearly purchased by his land's perdition.

These stanzas express a profound truth, though it is one oftener found in Eastern than in Western philosophy. Byron would have agreed with Chuang Tzu: 'The last thing you should do is to tamper with men's hearts. The heart of man is like a spring; if you press it down, it only springs up the higher.' Or, in words more familiar but still of Eastern origin: 'Which of you by taking thought can add one cubit unto his stature.' Properly speaking, satire is not an instrument of moral reform, or does not need to be; it is a mirror held up to the absurd or vicious aspects of human nature. The poet's role ends with that action. Byron's charge against Cervantes is that he made sport of 'noblest views'. It can be argued that this was not Cervantes's own intention—that it is merely the way the world has taken him.

There remains a whole section of Byron's work, not satirical in intention, and perhaps for this reason neglected by critics—those works of his last years which were to constitute what he called 'a mental theatre'. They begin, in 1817, with *Manfred*. *Marino Faliero* followed in 1820, and then, in rapid succession, *Sardanapalus* (January–May 1821), *The Two Foscari* (June–July 1821), *Cain* (July–September 1821), *Heaven and Earth* (October 1821), *Werner* (December 1821–January 1822), *The Deformed Transformed* (May–June 1822). *Manfred* lies apart, not only in date, but also in substance and style. Its similarity to Marlowe's *Doctor Faustus* and Goethe's *Faust* has often been remarked, but is rather difficult to account for—Goethe was pleased to recognize his parentage, but Byron more than once protested that he had never read or seen Marlowe's play and only knew Goethe's 'from a sorry French translation, from an occasional reading or two into English of parts of it by Monk Lewis when at Diodati, and from the Hartz mountain-scene, that Shelley versified the other day'. (Medwin, *Conversations* (1824), p. 170.) The last remark is the most significant one, for in style and spirit *Manfred* belongs to Shelley's rather than to Goethe's world. In the year preceding its composition the two poets had been thrown together at a critical moment in both their lives, and they had become very intimate. Shelley's influence on Byron was direct and deep, and *Manfred* springs from the same poetic atmosphere as *Julian and Maddalo* and *Prometheus Unbound*. It has all Shelley's expressive energy, but it lacks his subtle fire. Even the soliloquy that Goethe admired so much ('We are the Fools of Time and Terror') is sullen metal. It is different when Byron interpolates an Incantation such as the lines beginning:

> When the Moon is on the wave,
> And the glow-worm in the grass

for although these are essentially Shelleyan in style, they take on an exceptional intensity because Byron is really addressing his sister Augusta and calling down a curse on his wife Annabella:

> By the cold breast and serpent smile,
> By thy unfathomed gulfs of guile,
> By that most seeming virtuous eye,
> By thy shut soul's hypocrisy;
> By the perfection of thine art
> Which passed for human thine own heart;
> By thy delight in others' pain,
> And by thy brotherhood of Cain,
> I call upon thee! and compel
> Thyself to be thy proper Hell!

With *Marino Faliero* began an altogether different type of drama, without parallel unless it is in the French theatre of our own time (I am thinking of certain plays of Giraudoux, Montherlant, and Camus). Byron was fairly explicit about his intentions: 'Your friend', he writes to Murray (23 August 1821) 'is not aware, that my dramatic simplicity is *studiously* Greek, and must continue so: *no* reform ever succeeded at first. I admire the old English dramatists; but this is quite another field, and has nothing to do with theirs. I want to make a *regular* English drama, no matter whether for the Stage or not, which is not my object,—but a *mental theatre.*' And again, about a month later (20 September) to the same correspondent: 'I am much mortified that Gifford don't take to my new dramas: to be sure, they are as opposite to the English drama as one thing can be to another; but I have a notion that, if understood, they will in time find favour (though *not* on the stage) with the reader. The Simplicity of plot is intentional, and the avoidance of *rant* also, as also the compression of the Speeches in the more severe situations.' Here again Byron is showing himself the classicist. By a 'regular' English drama, he means a drama that pays strict attention to the dramatic unities. Earlier in this same year Byron had had his passionate controversy with the Rev. W. L. Bowles on the life and writings of Pope. This had driven him to consider in some detail what Mr. Bowles had called 'the invariable principles of poetry', and he had reached the remarkable conclusion that Pope 'is the moral poet of all civilization; and as such, let us hope that he will one day be the national poet of mankind. He is the only poet that never shocks; the only poet whose *faultlessness* has been made his reproach.' Now Pope, in the variety of his work, had never attempted drama, and I think it likely that Byron, in order to prove the validity of Pope's ideals in all categories of poetry, had the ambition to fill this niche in the classical façade.

Of the later group of plays, *Cain* is the only one that has received much attention from posterity. The dramatic nature of its theme, in which some reference to Byron's own dilemmas is not far to seek, and its challenge to conventional piety, all contributed to the opinion expressed by Scott— that Byron had 'certainly matched Milton on his own ground'. But that was not Byron's intention, and I doubt if he ever had Milton in mind in the writing of *Cain*, though he afterwards used Milton's example to defend himself against the charge of blasphemy. His aim, as Goethe recognized, was simply to dramatize an incident from the Old Testament; and a similar aim prevailed in his historical dramas, *Sardanapalus* and *The Two Foscari*. The latter Byron himself regarded as his best drama, and it certainly best exhibits the characteristic features of his mental theatre— dramatic unity and historical accuracy. To this latter quality

Byron attached what may seem to us undue importance; but that was his aesthetic 'problem'—to take the facts and reduce them to 'dramatic regularity'. To bring an historical event into sharp dramatic focus seemed to him to offer new possibilities to an outworn convention.

Heaven and Earth seems to be another product of Shelley's influence—not in its subject-matter, which is again Biblical, but in its choral style. It was never completed. Shelley's influence is evident again in *The Deformed Transformed*. Shelley thought it was 'a bad imitation of *Faust*', and it too was never completed. The last complete drama, *Werner*, is the most curious of all Byron's works—even its genuineness has been doubted, though without proof.[1] It is difficult to see what attracted Byron to this 'German's Tale' published in Lee's *Canterbury Tales*; it is a story of murder and violence —'a son pre-destined to evil by the weakness and sensuality of his father, a father punished for his want of rectitude by the passionate criminality of his son'. One can only suppose that Byron thought it was a good subject to exercise his new-found talents on, but the result bears all the marks of haste and impatience. Yet the story held some particular fascination for Byron. 'When I was young,' he writes in the Preface, '(about fourteen I think,) I first read this tale, which made a deep impression on me; and may, indeed, be said to contain the germ of much that I have since written.' With this lead, it might be possible, with diligence, to discover some psychological significance in it all; it would be more difficult to discover any poetic beauty.

During these two years of feverish dramatic activity, there is no doubt that the inner compulsion, which lay behind all his writing, reached its climacteric. It was a bored lover and exhausted poet that set sail for Greece on 13 July 1823 to seek in action the redemption he had not found in thought.

---

[1] In the *Nineteenth Century*, August 1899, the Hon. F. Leveson Gower attempted to prove that it was written by Georgiana, Duchess of Devonshire. E. H. Coleridge effectively refutes this theory in vol. V of *The Works of Lord Byron*.

There is at the base of all Byron's work an essential sanity, a hatred of sham and humbug, generous impulses and manly courage. His virtues may not correspond to the conventional code—as I have said, he was a free spirit, and if we cannot all be free spirits, at least it is good that once at least in a generation there should be a poet who rises above the daily conflict of vice and virtue to view the spectacle with cynical humour.

> Pythagoras, Locke, Socrates—but pages
>   Might be filled up, as vainly as before,
> With the sad usage of all sorts of sages,
>   Who in his life-time, each, was deemed a Bore!
> The loftiest minds outrun their tardy ages:
>   This must they bear with and, perhaps, much more;
> The wise man's sure when he no more can share it, he
> Will have a firm Post Obit on posterity.
>
> If such doom waits each intellectual Giant,
>   We little people in our lesser way,
> In Life's small rubs should surely be more pliant,
>   And so for one will I—as well I may—
> Would that I were less bilious—but, oh, fie on 't!
>   Just as I make my mind up every day,
> To be a '*totus, teres*', Stoic, Sage,
> The wind shifts and I fly into a rage.
>
> Temperate I am—yet never had a temper;
>   Modest I am—yet with some slight assurance;
> Changeable too—yet somehow '*Idem semper*':
>   Patient—but not enamoured of endurance;
> Cheerful—but, sometimes, rather apt to whimper:
>   Mild—but at times a sort of '*Hercules furens*':
> So that I almost think that the same skin
> For one without—has two or three within.

These were among the fourteen stanzas of a Seventeenth Canto of *Don Juan* found by Trelawny in Byron's room at Missolonghi. They might well remain as his epitaph.

BYRON

A Select Bibliography

(Place of publication London, unless stated otherwise.)

Bibliographies:

[BIBLIOGRAPHY by J. P. Anderson] in *The Life of Lord Byron*, by Hon. R. Noel (1890).
Contains extensive lists of magazine articles about Byron and of musical settings.

A BIBLIOGRAPHY OF SUCCESSIVE EDITIONS AND TRANSLATIONS in *The Works of Lord Byron. Poetry, vol. VII* (1904), ed. E. H. Coleridge.
The best general bibliography of the poems.

BYRON IN ENGLAND, by S. C. Chew (1924).
Contains an extensive list of Byroniana.

BIBLIOGRAPHICAL CATALOGUE of the First Editions, Proof Copies and Manuscripts of Books by Lord Byron, Exhibited at the First Edition Club, January 1925 (1925).

BYRON AND BYRONIANA. A Catalogue of Books (1930).
An important catalogue, valuable for reference, issued by Elkin Mathews, the London booksellers.

A BIBLIOGRAPHY OF THE WRITINGS IN VERSE AND PROSE OF GEORGE GORDON NOEL, BARON BYRON. With Letters illustrating his Life and Work and particularly his attitude towards Keats, by T. J. Wise. 2 vols. (1932–3).
The standard technical bibliography. Incorporates the material of the same author's *A Byron Library*, 1928—the privately printed catalogue of the Byron Collection in the Ashley Library, now in the British Museum.

THE ROE-BYRON COLLECTION, Newstead Abbey. Nottingham (1937).
The catalogue of the collection at Byron's ancestral home.

Note: The archives of John Murray, Byron's publishers, at 50 Albemarle Street, London, contain important manuscript material.

Collected Editions (a selection):

THE POETICAL WORKS, 2 vols. Philadelphia (1813).
The first collected edition, followed throughout the nineteenth century by numerous other collected editions in several volumes, published in London, Paris, New York, and elsewhere.

THE WORKS, 8 vols. (1815–20).

THE WORKS, 6 vols. (1829).

THE WORKS, with His Letters and Journals, and His Life, by Thomas Moore. Edited by J. Wright. 17 vols. (1832–3).

THE ILLUSTRATED BYRON with over 200 Engravings from Original Drawings, by Kennedy Meadows, Birket Foster, etc. (1854–5). Issued in parts.

THE POETICAL WORKS. New Edition, with the Text Carefully Revised. 6 vols. (1857).

THE POETICAL WORKS, Edited, with a Critical Memoir, by W. M. Rossetti. Illustrated by Ford Madox Brown. 8 vols. (1870).

THE WORKS. A New, Revised, and Enlarged Edition with Illustrations, including Portraits. 13 vols. (1898–1904).
Poetry, edited by E. H. Coleridge, 7 vols. *Letters and Journals*, edited by R. H. Prothero, 6 vols.

THE POETICAL WORKS. The Only Complete and Copyright Text in 1 vol. Edited, with a Memoir, by E. H. Coleridge (1905).
The standard edition, published by John Murray and often reprinted.

Note: Many anthologies of Byron's poems have been made, notably the selections of Matthew Arnold (1881); A. C. Swinburne (1885); H. J. C. Grierson (1923); E. Rhys (1927); J. Bennett (1937); P. Quennell (Nonesuch Ed. 1949).

Separate Works in verse:

FUGITIVE PIECES [Newark, 1806].
Privately printed and anonymous. Facsimile reprint, ed. H. B. Forman (1886).

POEMS ON VARIOUS OCCASIONS, Newark (1807).
Privately printed and anonymous.

HOURS OF IDLENESS: A Series of Poems Original and Translated, Newark (1807).

ENGLISH BARDS AND SCOTCH REVIEWERS. A Satire [1809].
The early editions of this poem were frequently counterfeited.

ADDRESS WRITTEN BY LORD BYRON. The Genuine Rejected Addresses, Presented to the Committee of Management for Drury Lane Theatre: Preceded by that written by Lord Byron and adopted by the Committee (1812).

SELECT BIBLIOGRAPHY

CHILDE HAROLD'S PILGRIMAGE. A Romaunt. Cantos I and II (1812). Canto III was published in 1816, Canto IV in 1818; Cantos I-IV were collected in 2 vols. (1819).

THE CURSE OF MINERVA. A Poem. (1812).

WALTZ. An Apostrophic Hymn 'by Horace Hornem, Esq.' (1813).

THE GIAOUR. A Fragment of a Turkish Tale (1813).

THE BRIDE OF ABYDOS. A Turkish Tale (1813).

THE CORSAIR. A Tale (1814).

ODE TO NAPOLEON BUONAPARTE (1814).
Anonymous.

LARA. A Tale. JACQUELINE. A Tale (1814).

HEBREW MELODIES, Ancient and Modern with appropriate Symphonies and Accompaniments (1815).

THE SIEGE OF CORINTH. A Poem. PARISINA. A Poem (1816).
Anonymous.

[POEMS ON HIS DOMESTIC CIRCUMSTANCES] (i. Fare Thee Well. ii. A Sketch from Private Life) (1816).
These two poems had been privately printed and separately printed in the same year. Various editions of this collection with additional poems were published in 1816.

POEMS (1816).

THE PRISONER OF CHILLON AND OTHER POEMS (1816).

MONODY ON THE DEATH OF THE RIGHT HON. R. B. SHERIDAN. Written at the Request of a Friend, to be Spoken at Drury Lane (1816).

THE LAMENT OF TASSO (1817).

MANFRED. A Dramatic Poem (1817).

BEPPO. A Venetian Story (1818).
Anonymous.

MAZEPPA. A Poem (1819).

DON JUAN. Cantos I and II (1819).
Cantos III, IV, V (1821); Cantos VI, VII, VIII (1823); Cantos IX, X, XI (1823); Cantos XII, XIII, XIV (1823); Cantos XV, XVI (1824). [All originally published anonymously.] First collected edition, 2 vols. (1826).

MARINO FALIERO, DOGE OF VENICE. An Historical Tragedy. THE PROPHECY OF DANTE. A Poem (1821).

SARDANAPALUS. A Tragedy. THE TWO FOSCARI. A Tragedy. CAIN. A Mystery (1821).

THE VISION OF JUDGMENT (1822). A product of Byron's feud with Southey, first printed in *The Liberal*, 1822, an ephemeral paper promoted by Byron and Leigh Hunt. Published as *The Two Visions* with Southey's 'Vision of Judgment' in the same year.

HEAVEN AND EARTH. A Mystery. Paris (1823).
Anonymous. First printed in *The Liberal*, 1823.

THE AGE OF BRONZE: Or, Carmen Seculare et Annus haud Mirabilis (1823).
Anonymous.

THE ISLAND: Or Christian and His Comrades (1823).

WERNER. A Tragedy (1823).

THE DEFORMED TRANSFORMED. A Drama (1824).

Separate Works in Prose:

LETTER TO [John Murray] ON THE REV. W. L. BOWLES' STRICTURES ON THE LIFE AND WRITINGS OF POPE (1821).

THE PARLIAMENTARY SPEECHES OF LORD BYRON. Printed from the Copies prepared by his Lordship for Publication (1824).

CORRESPONDENCE OF LORD BYRON WITH A FRIEND, including his Letters to his Mother in 1809-11. Edited by A. R. C. Dallas. 3 vols. Paris (1825).

LETTERS AND JOURNALS OF LORD BYRON, with Notices of his Life, by T. Moore. 2 vols. (1830, revised edition 1875).

LETTERS AND JOURNALS, edited by R. E. Prothero, 6 vols. (1898-1904).

POEMS AND LETTERS, edited from the original MSS. in the possession of W. K. Bixby, by W. N. C. Carlton. Chicago (1912).
Privately printed.

LORD BYRON'S CORRESPONDENCE, chiefly with Lady Melbourne, Mr. Hobhouse, the Hon. Douglas Kinnaird, and P. B. Shelley. Edited by John Murray. 2 vols. (1922).

SELECTED LETTERS, edited by V. H. Collins. Oxford (1928).

LETTERS. Edited by R. G. Howarth with an Introduction by André Maurois (1933).
Everyman's Library edition.

SELECT BIBLIOGRAPHY

THE RAVENNA JOURNAL, mainly Compiled at Ravenna in 1821, with an Introduction by Lord Ernle [R. E. Prothero] (1928). Printed for the members of the First Edition Club.

BYRON LETTERS AND DIARIES. A SELF-PORTRAIT. Edited by P. Quennell. 2 vols. (1950).
The largest and best selection of Byron's correspondence, including many hitherto unpublished letters.

Some Critical and Biographical Studies:

MEMOIRS OF THE LIFE AND WRITINGS OF THE RT. HON. LORD BYRON, with Anecdotes of Some of his Contemporaries, by [J. Watkins] (1822).

JOURNAL OF THE CONVERSATIONS OF LORD BYRON: Noted during a Residence with his Lordship at Pisa, in the Years 1821 and 1822, by T. Medwin (1824).

NOTES ON CAPTAIN MEDWIN'S CONVERSATIONS OF LORD BYRON, by John Murray (1824).
Privately printed. Reprinted in *Works*, 1829.

LORD BYRON, by L. S. Belloc. 2 vols. Paris (1824).

RECOLLECTIONS OF THE LIFE OF LORD BYRON, from the Year 1808 to the End of 1814, by R. C. Dallas (1824).

LETTERS ON THE CHARACTER AND POETICAL GENIUS OF LORD BYRON, by Sir S. E. Brydges (1824).

THE LIFE AND GENIUS OF LORD BYRON, by Sir C. Gordon (1824).

AN INQUIRY INTO THE MORAL CHARACTER OF LORD BYRON, by J. W. Simmons. New York (1824).

THE LAST DAYS OF LORD BYRON: With his Lordship's Opinions on Various Subjects, particularly on the State and Prospects of Greece, by Major W. Parry (1825).

AN IMPARTIAL PORTRAIT OF LORD BYRON AS A POET AND A MAN, by Sir S. E. Brydges. Paris (1825).

A NARRATIVE OF LORD BYRON'S LAST JOURNEY TO GREECE, by Count P. Gamba (1825).

ANECDOTES OF LORD BYRON FROM AUTHENTIC SOURCES, by [Alexander Kilgour] (1825).

NARRATIVE OF A SECOND VISIT TO GREECE, including Facts connected with the Last Days of Lord Byron. Extracts from Correspondence, Official Documents, etc. Edited by Edward Blaquiere (1825).

MEMOIRS OF THE LIFE AND WRITINGS OF LORD BYRON, by G. Cinton (1825).

THE LIFE, WRITINGS, OPINIONS AND TIMES OF THE RT. HON. GEORGE GORDON NOEL BYRON, LORD BYRON. By an English Gentleman in the Greek Military Service, and Comrade of his Lordship. Compiled from Authentic Documents and from Long Personal Acquaintance. 3 vols. (1825).
Ascribed to Matthew Iley.

A REVIEW OF THE CHARACTER AND WRITINGS OF LORD BYRON, by W. Phillips (1826).

THE LIFE OF LORD BYRON, by J. W. Lake. Paris (1826).

LORD BYRON AND SOME OF HIS CONTEMPORARIES, by Leigh Hunt (1828).

THE LIFE OF LORD BYRON, by J. Galt (1830).

CONVERSATIONS ON RELIGION WITH LORD BYRON AND OTHERS, by J. Kennedy (1830).

MEMOIRS OF THE AFFAIRS OF GREECE, with Various Anecdotes Relating to Lord Byron, and an Account of his Last Illness and Death, by J. Millingen (1831).

CONVERSATIONS OF LORD BYRON WITH THE COUNTESS OF BLESSINGTON, by Marguerite Gardiner, Countess of Blessington (1834).

FUNERAL ORATION DELIVERED AT MISSOLONGHI, April 1824, in Honour of the late Lord Byron, by S. Tricoupi (1836).
An English translation of the Greek original.

RECOLLECTIONS OF THE LAST DAYS OF SHELLEY AND BYRON, by E. J. Trelawny (1858; new ed., edited E. Dowden, 1906).
See also the same author's *Records of Shelley, Byron, and the Author*, 2 vols., 1878, new ed. 1905.

A VINDICATION OF LORD BYRON, by A. Austin (1869).

BYRON PAINTED BY HIS COMPEERS: Or, All about Lord Byron from his Marriage to his Death (1869).

LORD BYRON JUGÉ PAR LES TÉMOINS DE SA VIE, par Countess T. Guiccioli. 2 vols. (1868).
English translation, 1869.

MEDORA LEIGH. A History and An Autobiography, by E. M. Leigh. Edited by C. Mackay (1869).

SELECT BIBLIOGRAPHY

A CONTEMPORARY ACCOUNT OF THE SEPARATION OF LORD AND LADY BYRON: Also of the Destruction of Lord Byron's Memoirs, by J. C. Hobhouse (1870).
Privately printed. Reprinted in Hobhouse's *Recollections of a Long Life*.

BYRON, by J. Nichol (1880).
In the *English Men of Letters* series.

THE REAL LORD BYRON. New Views of the Poet's Life, by J. C. Jeaffreson. 2 vols. (1883).

BYRON RE-STUDIED IN HIS DRAMAS. An Essay. By W. Gerard [Smith] (1886).

THE LIFE OF LORD BYRON, by the Hon. R. Noel (1890).

LAST LINKS WITH BYRON, SHELLEY AND KEATS, by W. Graham (1898).

JOURNAL OF EDWARD ELLERKER WILLIAMS, Companion of Shelley and Byron in 1821 and 1822. With an Introduction by R. Garnett (1902).

IL GENERALE MENGALDO, LORD BYRON E L'ODE 'On the Star of the Legion of Honour'. Con un Saggio de Bibliografia Byroniana, di A. Lumbroso, Rome (1903).

LA FAMA DEL BYRON E IL BYRONISMO IN ITALIA, di G. Muoni, Milan (1903).
See also the same author's *La Leggenda del Byron in Italia*, Milan, 1907.

HEINRICH HEINE'S VERHALTNIS ZU LORD BYRON, by F. Melchoir, Weimar (1903).

ASTARTE. A Fragment of Truth concerning Lord Byron, by Ralph Milbanke, Earl of Lovelace (1905).
Privately printed. Enlarged edition, published 1921.

BYRON AND BYRONISM IN AMERICA. By W. E. Leonard, Boston, Mass. (1905).

LORD BYRON AND HIS DETRACTORS. *Astarte. Lord Byron and Lord Lovelace* by Sir J. Murray; *Lord Lovelace on the Separation of Lord and Lady Byron*, by R. E. Prothero (1906).
Privately printed for members of the Roxburghe Club.

BYRON: THE LAST PHASE, by R. J. F. Edgcumbe (1909).

LORD BYRON A VENEZIA, di N. Meneghetti, Venice [1910].

THE PILGRIM POET, LORD BYRON OF NEWSTEAD, by A. Brecknock (1911).

THE DIARY OF DR. JOHN WILLIAM POLIDORI, relating to Byron, etc. Edited and elucidated by W. M. Rossetti (1911).

THE LAST ILLNESS OF LORD BYRON, by J. Knott. St. Paul, Minn. (1912).

BYRON, by E. Colburn Mayne. 2 vols. (1912, new ed. 1924).
See also the same author's *The Life and Letters of Lady Noel Byron*, 1929.

LORD BYRON'S LAMENESS. The Correspondence of G. G. Napier and J. Ward. Edited by J. Ward, Nottingham (1915).
Privately printed.

THE DRAMAS OF LORD BYRON. A Critical Study by S. C. Chew, Göttingen (1915).

LORD BYRON'S ILLNESS AND DEATH as described in a Letter to the Hon. Augusta Leigh, dated from Missolonghi April 20, 1824, by W. Fletcher. Nottingham (1920).
Privately printed.

THE RELATIONS OF LORD BYRON AND AUGUSTA LEIGH. With a Comparison of the Characters of Byron and Shelley. Four letters by E. J. Trelawny (1920).
Privately printed.

BYRON IN ENGLAND: His Fame and After Fame, by S. C. Chew (1924).

BYRON, 1788–1824, par E. Rodocanachi, Paris [1924].

BYRON THE MAN, by R. L. Bellamy (1924).

BYRON. THE LAST JOURNEY, April 1823–April 1824, by the Hon. Harold Nicolson (1924, new ed. 1948).

BYRON IN PERSPECTIVE, by J. D. Symon [1924].

BYRON, THE POET. A Centenary Volume. Edited by W. A. Briscoe (1924).
A collection of addresses and essays, illustrated by portraits and facsimiles.

THE BYRON MYSTERY, by Sir J. C. Fox (1924).

BYRON AND GREECE, by E. H. Spender (1924).

THE POLITICAL CAREER OF LORD BYRON, by D. N. Raymond [1924].

THE PILGRIM OF ETERNITY: BYRON—A CONFLICT, by J. Drinkwater [1925].

SELECT BIBLIOGRAPHY 43

LA FORTUNA DI BYRON IN INGHILTERRA, di M. Praz, Florence (1925).

LA PRIMA DIMORA DI LORD BYRON A BOLOGNA, di F. Cantoni, Bologna (1926).
See also the same author's *Byron e la Guiccioli a Bologna*, Bologna, 1927.

ALLEGRA. The Story of Byron and Miss Clairmont, by A. C. Gordon. New York (1926).

LORD BYRON E P.B.SHELLEY A RAVENNA, E TERESA GUICCIOLI GAMBA, di L. Rava. Rome (1929).

BYRON, ET LE BESOIN DE LA FATALITÉ, par C. Du Bos, Paris (1929). English translation by E. Colburn Mayne, 1932.

BYRON, par André Maurois. 2 vols. Paris (1930). English translation by H. Miles, 1930.

BYRON, par M. Castelain, Paris (1931).

BYRON, by P. Quennell (1934).
A volume in Duckworth's *Brief Lives* series.

BYRON. THE YEARS OF FAME, by P. Quennell (1935).

ALLEGRA, by I. Origo (1935).

BYRON AS SKEPTIC AND BELIEVER, by E. W. Marjarum, Princeton, N.J. (1938).

TO LORD BYRON. Feminine Profiles, Based upon Unpublished Letters 1807-1824, by G. Paston and P. Quennell (1939).

BYRON IN ITALY, by P. Quennell (1941).

THE LIFE AND WORK OF LORD BYRON, by D. Gray. Nottingham (1945).

LORD BYRON'S FIRST PILGRIMAGE, by W. A. Borst. New Haven, Conn. (1948).

BYRON AND SWITZERLAND, by H. Straumann. Nottingham (1948).

THE LAST ATTACHMENT. The Story of Byron and Teresa Guiccioli, by I. Origo (1949).

BYRON AND SHELLEY, by D. G. James (1951).

GOETHE AND BYRON, by E. M. Butler (1951).

LORD BYRON, by G. W. Knight (1952).

BYRON'S DRAMATIC PROSE, by G. W. Knight (1953).

WRITERS AND THEIR WORK

JANE AUSTEN*: Sylvia Townsend Warner
HILAIRE BELLOC: Renée Haynes
ARNOLD BENNETT*: Frank Swinnerton
WILLIAM BLAKE*: Kathleen Raine
ELIZABETH BOWEN: Jocelyn Brooke
THE BRONTË SISTERS: Phyllis Bentley
SAMUEL BUTLER: G. D. H. Cole
THOMAS CARLYLE*: David Gascoyne
JOYCE CARY: Walter Allen
G. J. CHESTERTON: Christopher Hollis
COLERIDGE: Kathleen Raine
R. G. COLLINGWOOD: E. W. F. Tomlin
I. COMPTON-BURNETT*: Pamela Hansford Johnson
JOSEPH CONRAD: Oliver Warner
CHARLES DICKENS: K. J. Fielding
DEFOE: J. R. Sutherland
GEORGE ELIOT*: Lettice Cooper
T. S. ELIOT*: M. C. Bradbrook
FIELDING: John Butt
E. M. FORSTER: Rex Warner
CHRISTOPHER FRY: Derek Stanford
JOHN GALSWORTHY: R. H. Mottram
THOMAS HARDY*: R. A. Scott-James
G. M. HOPKINS: Geoffrey Grigson
ALDOUS HUXLEY: Jocelyn Brooke
HENRY JAMES: Michael Swan
SAMUEL JOHNSON: S. C. Roberts
JOHN KEATS: Edmund Blunden

RUDYARD KIPLING*: Bonamy Dobrée
CHARLES LAMB: Edmund Blunden
D. H. LAWRENCE: Kenneth Young
KATHERINE MANSFIELD: Ian A. Gordon
WALTER DE LA MARE: Kenneth Hopkins
JOHN MASEFIELD*: L. A. G. Strong
SOMERSET MAUGHAM*: John Brophy
MILTON: E. M. W. Tillyard
WILLIAM MORRIS: Philip Henderson
GEORGE ORWELL: Tom Hopkinson
POPE: Ian Jack
HERBERT READ: Francis Berry
BERTRAND RUSSELL*: Alan Dorward
BERNARD SHAW*: A. C. Ward
SHAKESPEARE: C. J. Sisson
SHELLEY: Stephen Spender
SHERIDAN*: W. A. Darlington
EDITH SITWELL: John Lehmann
OSBERT SITWELL*: Roger Fulford
TOBIAS SMOLLETT*: Laurence Brander
STERNE: D. W. Jefferson
R. L. STEVENSON: G. B. Stern
SWINBURNE: H. J. C. Grierson
G. M. TREVELYAN*: J. H. Plumb
EVELYN WAUGH: Christopher Hollis
H. G. WELLS: Montgomery Belgion
OSCAR WILDE: James Laver
VIRGINIA WOOLF: Bernard Blackstone
WORDSWORTH: Helen Darbishire
W. B. YEATS: G. S. Fraser

Available at 2s. net each; starred titles 1s. 6d. net each

¶ Essays in active preparation include: *Swift* by J. Middleton Murry, and assessments of Izaak Walton, Gibbon, Wyndham Lewis, Graham Greene, C. Day **Lewis** and other classics and contemporaries.

WRITERS AND THEIR WORK

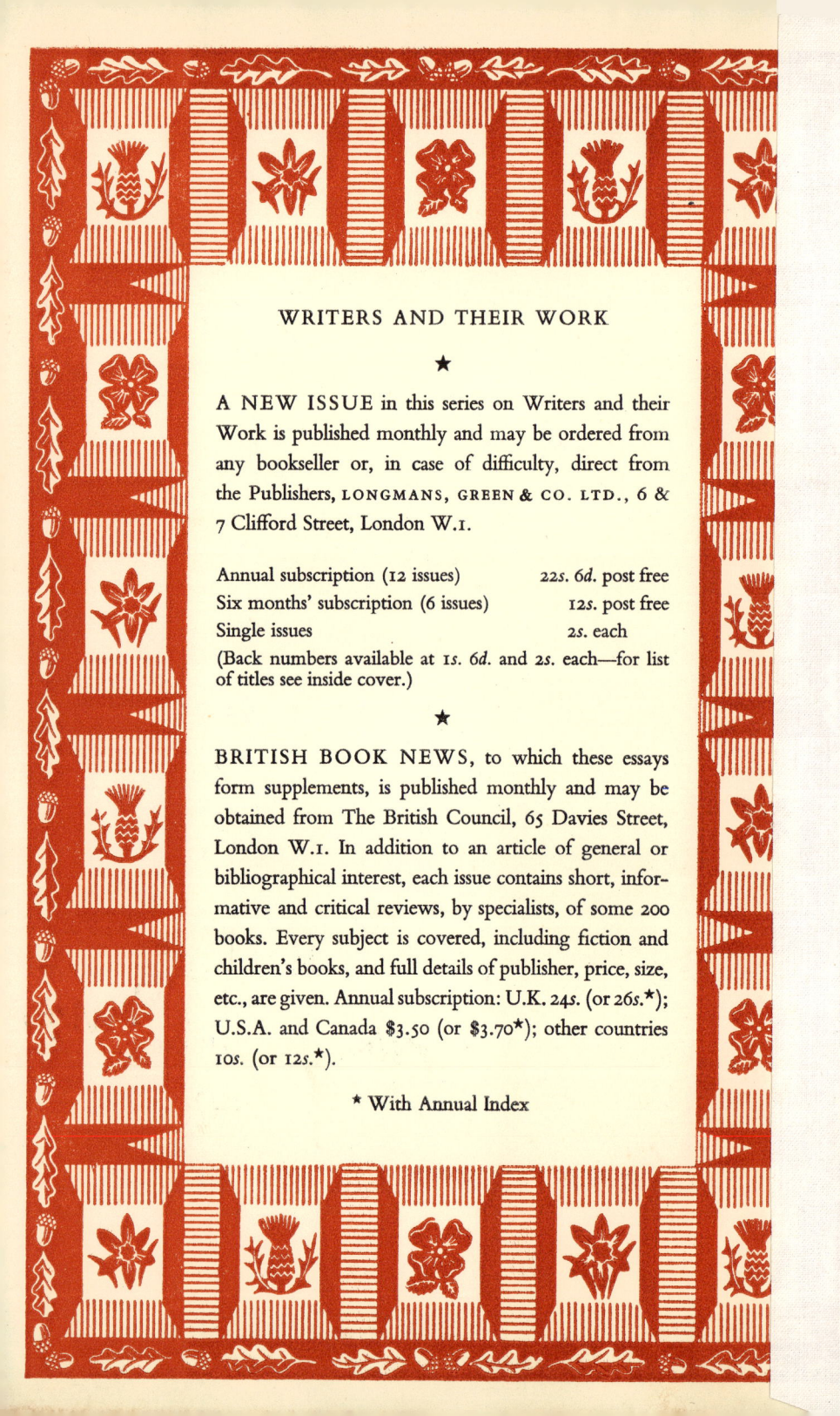

★

A NEW ISSUE in this series on Writers and their Work is published monthly and may be ordered from any bookseller or, in case of difficulty, direct from the Publishers, LONGMANS, GREEN & CO. LTD., 6 & 7 Clifford Street, London W.1.

Annual subscription (12 issues)	22s. 6d. post free
Six months' subscription (6 issues)	12s. post free
Single issues	2s. each

(Back numbers available at 1s. 6d. and 2s. each—for list of titles see inside cover.)

★

BRITISH BOOK NEWS, to which these essays form supplements, is published monthly and may be obtained from The British Council, 65 Davies Street, London W.1. In addition to an article of general or bibliographical interest, each issue contains short, informative and critical reviews, by specialists, of some 200 books. Every subject is covered, including fiction and children's books, and full details of publisher, price, size, etc., are given. Annual subscription: U.K. 24s. (or 26s.★); U.S.A. and Canada $3.50 (or $3.70★); other countries 10s. (or 12s.★).

★ With Annual Index